Are You The ARCHITECT of Your CIRCUMSTANCES?

How the QUALITY of your THOUGHTS and CHOICES shape your CIRCUMSTANCES

★★★★★ Rated Five Stars By Forbes.com (2006)

Candido Segarra

www.ForesightPublishingNow.com

Copyright © 2004, 2010 Foresight Publishing Group

Are You The Architect of Your Circumstances

by: Candido Segarra

www.foresightpublishingnow.com/candido

Printed in the United States of America

ISBN 0-9844423-0-8

All rights reserved solely by the author. The author guarantees all contents are original and do not infringe upon the legal rights of any other person or work. No part of this book may be reproduced in any form without the permission of the author. The views expressed in this book are not necessarily those of the publisher.

Unless otherwise indicated, Bible quotations are taken from New International Version by Tyndale House Publishers, Inc. and Zondervan Publishing House. Copyright © 1973, 1978, 1984, by The International Bible Society

www.foresightpublishingnow.com

To My Beloved Wife Cathy

Whose joy for life, love, support and dedication has given stability to my life and enable me to risk, grow, and experience life without fear. Your honest friendship, unconditional companionship and commitment, in spite of myself, have allowed me to grow spiritually and emotionally. Our life struggles together have brought us closer to God and to each other. My love for you will always be unconditional and eternal.

To My Beloved Children

I pray that someday, my character will be my legacy to you. You have taught me the real meaning of love. I hope that I will become the kind of father that God wants me to be for you and that you deserve.

To Michelle: I hope that this book will transform your life even in a small way. I miss you.

To Juan: You are my soul mate and the person of character I wished I had been at your age.

To Jorge: I pray that someday you will realize how special you are to me. I love you for who you are.

To Viviana: What a blessing and a godly young woman you are! My life has changed over the past years for the best because of you. I love you more than words can express.

To Katie: You light up my life. You are a gift and a blessing from God. You are teaching me lessons of love every day.

TABLE OF CONTENTS

DEDICATION

ACKNOWLEDGMENTS

FOREWORD IX

INTRODUCTION XIII

CHAPTER ONE .... MAN'S FREE WILL AND THE SOVEREIGNTY OF GOD 15
CHAPTER TWO .... THE RELATION BETWEEN THOUGHT AND CHARACTER-BUILDING ... 23
CHAPTER THREE .... THE END RESULT OF THOUGHT IN YOUR CIRCUMSTANCES 29
CHAPTER FOUR ..... MAN'S THOUGHTS AND CRISIS 43
CHAPTER FIVE ...... THE IMPACT OF THOUGHTS ON YOUR HEALTH AND BODY 47
CHAPTER SIX .... THOUGHT, PURPOSE AND DETERMINATION 51
CHAPTER SEVEN .... THE THOUGHT AND MOTIVE IN ACHIEVEMENT 55
CHAPTER EIGHT .... VISIONARY DREAMS 59
CHAPTER NINE ...... THE INNER SILENCE AND SUBMISSION TO GOD 65
CHAPTER TEN .... THE INNER CALM 67

PROLOGUE 71

WORKS CITED

Foreword

I have learned through studying history that individual and collective circumstances deteriorate when we ignore the absolute truth that everything begins and ends with God and that man, although free to choose, is only an instrument of God's glory. The deterioration reaches a point where morality, as defined by God, becomes wrong; and wrong, as defined by God, becomes socially right and acceptable, even a "civil right".

Years ago, I had a personal, spiritual encounter with God. Exhausted from the constant struggle to keep up in the "rat race" and devastated after losing my family and business to divorce and bankruptcy I was at the very lowest point of my existence. I was experiencing a crisis of identify and inner turmoil to which I had no other outlet of appeal but my Creator. The day that I recognized how far I was from God's goodness and character and decided to let God change my ways by submitting to His control in my life circumstances, He gave me an immense comfort, reassurance, inner strength and peace, that I had never before experienced in my life.

Through the study of and the power contained in God's Word, the Bible, God revealed Himself to me and showed me *His* character through Jesus the Christ. God gave me the model of the moral man, through which I can *become* like Him.

From that day forward, my life has drastically changed for the better. The acceptance of God's forgiveness and recognition of His sovereignty has proven to be the single most important choice I have ever made in my life.

This book does not promote the senseless philosophy that "man creates his own reality." On the contrary, through my own personal experience validated by what the Holy Bible reveals, I have learned that there is no true reality apart from God.

A few years ago as I studied the Scriptures, I found the following verse: *"As a man think in his heart, so is he"* (Proverbs 23:7 NKJ). I also found many other passages in the Bible addressing the renewal of the mind and the relationship between God, faith, thought and the circumstances of man. Those scriptures were like seeds planted in my mind, ready to evolve.

Are You The Architect Of Your Circumstances dissects the anatomy of our circumstances and reveals the power of God in relation to our choices. It is a sincere effort to be an instrument that God will use to inspire readers to be vigilant of their thoughts through the power that a renewed relationship with our Creator brings. The concepts shared here are influenced by a Judeo-Christian perspective and are a result of my own experiences and continuous search for new wisdom in the Truth of God's Word.

What perhaps makes this book a fascinating learning journey as well as an intimidating personal reflection is the idea that God has given us personal responsibility and the *power* of *choice*. We have the power to choose our thoughts and attitudes, which consequently will build our character and ultimately reflect in our circumstances.

Every action produce a reaction, as every sin has a consequence. Every good or bad deed and every thought, pure or impure, selfish or unselfish that we let grow in our minds will germinate in a similar condition in our life experience. This is to say that good actions bring back similar conditions in our lives, as bad actions will surface as bad experiences in our reality.

In God's infinite justice system it is impossible for injustice to occur, because God's spiritual laws have provided for automatic justice. Man automatically penalizes himself when committing a misdeed, as the misdeed returns to him in the form of unfavorable circumstances. Through this, God allows man the opportunity to "reverse" and understand good and unselfishness versus evil and selfishness so that he can learn to choose godly virtues.

Therefore, *every* circumstance is an opportunity to grow spiritually and to grow in our love for our fellowmen, showing God's unmerited forgiveness, grace, infinite love, mercy and justice.

Finally, but not less important; the word "man" is used in this book as a *generic* term, meaning *human* and the term "men" to describe, *humanity*. In no way is the term "man" or its plural meant to suggest gender.

I encourage you to read this book with an open mind and

heart. I hope that you will be able to experience a total transformation of your life by seeking God and allowing Him to unleash His power within you, through patience, meekness, humility and submission to Him.

It is only through His power that you will be able to transform your mind and your circumstances by becoming a sentinel of your thoughts, a guardian of your heart and most important, by submitting your life to God and persistently pursuing His Godly character.

CANDIDO SEGARRA

Introduction

This is a book about the connection between God, man and our circumstances. It is a study on the correlation between God and His grace; how men thought-choices shape our character and how our character molds our circumstances.

The reason for our existence is to glorify God by growing in His unconditional love as we become *like* Him. Through our thought-life, God permits us to experience and shape circumstances to help us learn and practice the lessons of love that will make us grow in any personal area where we may need spiritual development. Our thoughts are the seeds of our circumstances.

During our lifetime, God will present us with circumstances that, according to our thought-life, will give us the opportunity to learn and to choose love vs. hate; compassion vs. coldness; humility vs. pride; sharing vs. greed; service vs. disservice; kindness vs. unkindness; joy vs. sorrow; peace vs. disturbance; faithfulness vs. untruthfulness; goodness vs. badness; gentleness vs. rudeness; self-control vs. self-indulgence, etc., etc.

In the world of academia, we never advance to the next grade, unless the lessons of the previous grade are not fully learned. Each grade is foundational to understanding the next one and the degree of our success, under normal circumstances, is determined by our choices, attitudes (thought-life), discipline and persistence.

As in school, God will present us with circumstances through our lifetime to help us learn, practice, understand and move us on with the lessons that will make us grow in His nature and His love. However, as in school, we are given the choice to learn and grow, or not, and the quality of our lives reflects such choices.

The power to choose our most prevalent thoughts is ours to be tame. Our thoughts and actions are motivated either by love, or fear. Circumstances in any particular area will keep presenting themselves in different ways. They will be patterned after our thought-choices, until we have learned the lesson(s) contained in that particular set of circumstances, and we are ready to submit our will to God in order to be able to elevate the quality of our thoughts and move on to another area (or areas) in which we need spiritual growth.

You see, under this context, circumstances are not "bad;" they are all "good", unless you live your life separated from God (Romans 8:28 NIV). It is only through our separation from God's grace that we perceive and value-judge circumstances as "good" or "bad", as we are unable to see God's grace working through our circumstances. The more we get to know God, the more we will realize that every circumstance is an opportunity to learn and grow in His character. Every circumstance hides the seed of goodness and the fruit of God's Spirit.

If we trust God unconditionally, and if we seek His counsel, exchanging our self-sufficiency with His all-sufficient power, then our "Free will" is not that "free", as we *become* the will of God, turning into an instrument that God can use to work on His will and to shine His love through us. Through this constant state of submission, we gradually (throughout our lifetime) become what C.S. Lewis boldly described in his book Mere Christianity as "little Christ's", in character and actions.

My prayer for you is that, through your diligent pursue of Biblical truth, and by becoming a constant vigilant of your thoughts, you too will become a "little Christ"; an instrument of God's love, grace and mercy.

MAN'S FREE WILL AND THE SOVEREIGNTY OF GOD

If God is in control of everything, then what is man's responsibility in life? Where does man's free will fit-in? This has been the eternal discourse of men over the ages. In order to have a better understanding of men's choice and God's sovereignty, let's examine this apparent paradox.

God works *alongside* men, rather than in *control of* men, and He is also omnipresent - we cannot escape His presence (Psalm 139). He knows our secrets, desires and thoughts. Although He doesn't *force* Himself on us, in His *foreknowledge*, He already knows what we are going to choose. Nevertheless, in His *grace* and love, He can choose to intervene, *influence* and orchestrate circumstances that will usher us into lessons of love, which we must learn and practice, in order to become more *like* Him.

Therefore, there is a direct interrelationship and interaction between the *sovereignty* of God - God is in control of everything - and the self-centered action-choices we make, as we face our circumstances.

What are the origins of our self-centered nature? What makes us desire what is best for us, rather than what is best for the common good?

In Genesis 3 the Bible gives an account of the fall of men, where the first challenge and act of disobedience by a creature to his Creator was recorded. This account brings forth to the human experience the conflict between selfishness and disobedience versus unselfishness and submission to God. The bond of total oneness and unselfish love that Adam and Eve shared and enjoyed with their Creator was broken, starting humanity's selfish path of desiring to live a life *independent* from God. The moment they chose to compete with God, lusting for His attributes - wanting to be *like* God for their own benefit - they lost their identity as children of God and by heritage, humanity lost the *ability* to choose right (unselfishness) from wrong (selfishness).

As our ancestors became discontent with their circumstances, wanting to live life on their own terms and for their own selfish purposes (just like we do today), they chose to abandon the source of *love* by trying to become love on their own. Thus, *fear* and *doubt* were born into the world.

Seeking their own self-interest, they chose to exchange God's moral love-based standard, enjoyed through a relationship of oneness with Him, for a very limited man-made, self-seeking, fear-based standard. Because of his inheritance, a man will naturally choose self-interest. God's moral standards, which lead us to humility, submission and reverence to God as well as love, joy and unselfishness in our relationships, are not the result of men's will or natural choices, but of God's grace as He works His love *through* us. In our natural condition, we choose what we choose because it seems to us that it is right, good, beneficial, advantageous and proper for *us*. If we track the motives behind most of our decisions, we will recognize that in most cases, they are self-centered in nature. Our choices will always align with what seems good for *us* and the strongest inner motives (selfishness) will always determine our choices.

The reason we cannot resist choosing selfishness over unconditional love and unselfishness, is that we love *ourselves* too much and we *fear* to lose control over our lives. As a result, we find ourselves with no *power*, desire, or inclination to abandon our self-indulgent lives. Even when we think we are doing something "good" out of our own "self- power" and "goodness", if we look deep within ourselves and truly trace the motives for our actions, we will find that behind our "good" actions there is a self-serving purpose.

Take for example a person that is confronted with a decision of whether to have an extramarital affair. He may decide **not** to have an affair after considering the consequences that will undoubtedly result for him and his family. He may fear that his family's destruction will devastate *him* emotionally and everything *he* has worked for.

Although on the surface his decision appears to be considerate, noble and unselfish, his motives have more to do with *him* and the consequences *he* will have to face, than about his family.

Another example: a politician propagates a decision that appears to be for the best interest of his constituents through rationalization and "spinning" techniques. In reality, the decision is merely part of a strategy to further his own political agenda.

Again, though he appears altruistic through his actions, true reality reveals that the politician's motives are to advance his political career rather than to serve the common good.

Only through God's irresistible *gift* of faith are we *enabled* with the *power* and the *capacity* to change our selfish thought process and start the process of desiring and choosing what is best for the greater good versus pursuing our self-centered interests and fear-based choices. This ultimately marks the difference between a life demonstrating unconditional love or a shallow, unhappy existence.

In life, we will come upon many forks in the road were God gives us the choice to change our lives through a sincere submission to Him. Many times we choose to stay in the status-quo of a self-centered life, thus bringing more misery and suffering into our relationships, before we completely surrender our desire to control everything and everyone and submit ourselves to God's control. Such a choice is usually triggered by overall life dissatisfaction or a deep-life crisis.

At that crossroad, our ability to believe and submit to God will only come through God's irresistible *gift* of faith. This gift is irresistible because when God speaks, He speaks with an overpowering supernatural persuasion. It is irresistible because the choice is obvious: a life of misery through the pursuing of self-centered desires and thoughts, or a path of total love and oneness with God through an unconditional and unselfish existence. When we accept this overpowering gift by placing our life and trust in the hands of the one who created us, He will *empower* and *enable* us, by planting the desire for His moral laws of life, love and righteousness in our hearts, along with the *responsibility* and *ability* to obey these spiritual and moral laws. This spiritual and supernatural exchange between God and man leads a man to a transformed life. It is as if being "born again," emerging from a dark tunnel with a different outlook on life.

God is responsible for the *gift* of faith (seed) and we are responsible for accepting the gift of that new life from the giver of life Himself and nurturing that seed for growth. But the *desire* to change and to keep our spiritual lives growing by keeping a bond of intimacy with God is man's responsibility.

A man is significant only in the measure of his identification with God's character, which is developed in us as we believe what He promises to us in His Word, and as we fully trust and cooperate with Him - that is, to obey Him. Through this divine moment-by-moment submission process, our thoughts start shifting toward desiring God and His character and abhorring more-and-more, day-by-day, our own selfish nature, actions and self-centered thoughts.

In Mathew 11:28 NIV, we see a perfect example of the inter-relationship of God's sovereignty and the responsibility of man for active trust and cooperation: *"Come to me all who are weary and I will give you rest."* In this passage, God's promised action (giving us rest) is *preceded* by man's action (believing the Giver, *coming* in obedience to Him, and trusting that we have already received the rest He promises).

A good example of this law of the responsibility of men and the sovereignty of God is shown to us in nature. When we plant a seed, it will surely die if it doesn't have water or access to sunlight. In the same way, a man will surely die in the absence of adequate food supply or water. We provide water and sun to a plant and food and water to our bodies, as we know that the result of our cooperation (or the lack of it) with the laws of nature could be the difference between life and death. We know and recognize these laws in nature and cooperate with them for our self-preservation and survival, but seldom do we apply it to our own spiritual life.

As with the laws of nature, God plants His laws of life, love and righteousness in men's hearts as a seed. He also gives men the responsibility to tend the seed with water and light – that is, to obey His spiritual and moral laws. This, in turn, will transform a man's life through the reaping process.

When we start *believing* and *trusting* God, He gives us through faith, a supernatural understanding of the redeeming power of the death of Christ on the cross, by which man's past is forgiven, the present is supplied with power, and the future is full of light and hope, placing us on a path of learning to love both God and people, unconditionally and unselfishly.

God is sovereign. We are significant in the eyes of God, as we were created in His image and are a reflection of His character and creativity. One of God's attributes is foreknowledge - He sees the present, past and future as an eternal now. Just because God already knows the outcomes does not mean that we are exempt from cooperating with the mind of God in our present circumstance. Dr. Jerome Barrs, distinguished professor at Covenant Seminary in St. Louis, MO wrote in his book, *To Be Human, "We are not justified in saying that foreordaining means only that God knows what humans and devils will decide ahead of time. This implies that God merely confirms the choices of others, rather than acting to work out his own purposes"*

God makes plans for humanity and works them out in history according to His divine purposes, but men make choices which may or may not align with God's plans. Men can either cooperate with God's plans or resist and rebel against them, risking the consequences of violating His natural laws and plans. We are constantly making choices and seeing the results, often to our own shame. Most of the time, we do not even see the connection between our selfish actions and violations and its corresponding consequences.

How does prayer, meditating and connecting with God affect your thoughts? God has made ***believing in prayer*** a pre-condition for ***receiving***: *"Therefore I tell you, whatever you ask for in prayer, believe that you have received it, and it will be yours."* (Mark 11:24 NIV). Nevertheless, as Reverend Samuel Hart says, *"The Giver has the right to choose His own terms for His gifts"* (cited in Reimann 249).

God cannot give until a man asks. When a man asks that which harmonizes with God's purpose for him, God puts His process in motion, creating the essential character traits in man that were non-existent until asked for. As redemption forms the life of God in a man, it also manifests the circumstances which harmonize with that new life; and so, as a man thinks in his heart, *so he becomes.*

Prayer does not change things. Prayer changes man's heart, empowering him to change things. Contrary to the materialistic school of thought, a man does not control or change external circumstances; through man's reflection and prayer, God changes the way man *looks* at circumstances. God changes men's inner nature allowing him to change his attitudes, which in turn, change circumstances.

Through prayer and meditation on the truth and wisdom given to man through the Scriptures, we can connect to the mind of God to learn His plans for us. We can *harmonize* and team up with Him to fulfill His redemptive plans for us and mankind, to glorify Himself and make Himself known.

In man's prayers and petitions, God will either confirm our petition - through people, circumstances, prayer, a reading, etc. - or He will give us an alternate course of action to follow, perhaps through an insight, idea or an open door of opportunity. He may also include a *"don't do it," "not now"*, or *"move on"* answer. To desire and trust through prayer is to *obtain, as in the following scripture from John 15:7-8 NIV:* **"If you remain in me and my words remain in you, ask whatever you wish, and it will be given you. This is to my Father's glory, that you bear much fruit, showing yourselves to be my disciples."** To desire in prayer, if it conforms to God's will, glorifies Him and helps you bear fruit, is to obtain; prayer, aspiration, vision and submission to God is achievement.

We know we are cooperating with God's will when our decisions and actions conform to God's moral standards, thus, giving us a sense of peace. We know when we are resisting God's plan when we feel we are trying to put a "round peg in a square hole" and spend our time rationalizing our actions, even when we *know* our actions are selfish in nature and may not bear fruit for us, or glorify Him. Often we seek "wise counsel" only to try to obtain validation for what we have already decided to pursue anyway.

As we cooperate with God and restrain ourselves from acting selfishly and stubbornly independent of Him, God will develop in our character the fruits of love, joy, peace, patience, kindness, goodness, faithfulness, gentleness and self-control (Galatians 5:22-23 NIV), as well as the power to sustain that life.

This is not a passive process; it takes personal responsibility. As we recognize the need for an internal spiritual change at the same time as recognizing our personal responsibility of trusting Him to lead the *process*, the result can be spectacular spiritual growth and wisdom.

This is a moment-by-moment lifetime effort, as we trust and rest confidently in the empowerment that God is giving us through His Spirit to sustain the process and to persevere in the direction of God's plans and ways.

This shows how personal God is. He loves, understands and cherishes those whom He has made in His image. As Dr. Barrs perfectly expresses it: *"He is sovereign and yet he also recognizes that our nature, as persons made like him, is to will, decide and act."*

Without this understanding of the relationship between an action and its consequence and between God's actions and ours, there will be no real spiritual growth.

Man's will is made perfectly and immutably free to goodness *only* in the state of God's grace and power.

As God empowers a man to desire Him, and as a man submits in meekness and humility to the sovereignty and guidance of God, his faith will increase and the *power* to elevate the quality of his thoughts through prayer is granted, as what God desires is for us to align our thoughts with His own nature.

A man *has control over his attitudes and weakness.* If a man is not convinced of the part he plays in his own growth, then, God will hold him accountable for his own failures and its correspondent consequences, which will inevitably surface in man's circumstances, in order for him to learn the lessons of love. Life's ultimate love lesson is this: *"Love the Lord your God with all your heart and with all your soul and with all your mind...Love your neighbor as yourself."*(Mathew 22:37-39 NIV).

There is a tremendous strength acquired from honestly struggling with our actions, attitudes, weaknesses and selfishness. Our awareness and total confidence that God's Spirit is within us working in our character brings the realization that we are not alone and that God is actively working in our inner nature to change us as we grow in His likeness.

In summary, although God is in control of everything, he works in the natural world through men's choices, with outcomes that are influenced either by the selfish nature of people, or the unselfish nature of people.

It is through unselfish people that we see the reflection of who God is. That is why God came to this world in time and space in the *person* of Jesus, *which is the radiance of God's glory and the exact representation of His being* (Heb 1:3 NIV), so we can see who God *Is*, through the character of Jesus. We are created with the full potential to be *like* Jesus, the image of God, on earth.

THE RELATION BETWEEN THOUGHTS AND CHARACTER-BUILDING

We are spiritual beings existing in a material world. We are matter, soul and spirit. Our thoughts and emotions, our soul, are the essence of our character; what we think and feel is the result of our life experiences and the emotions associated with these experiences. What we believe, based on our emotional associations, shapes our circumstances.

Proverbs 23:7 states, *"As a man thinks in his heart so is he."* This truth not only involves the entirety of man's existence and character formation but also is so comprehensive as to touch every condition and circumstance in our lives.

A man and his character is literally the complete sum of his most prevalent thoughts and beliefs. His character shapes his circumstances. Our most prevalent thoughts will become our habits. Our beliefs and habits, good or bad, shape our character. Our character molds and mirrors our circumstances.

Change the way you think and you will change your life. Change is a *desire*, which always starts with a *choice* - selfish or unselfish - in a man's thoughts.

In the same way that a plant originates from and could not

exist without a seed, so every man's actions have its beginnings from the hidden seeds of his own thoughts. This applies equally to those actions that are called "spontaneous", "unpremeditated" or "subconscious" as to those which are deliberately, consciously and premeditatedly thought-out and executed.

Attitudes are the fruit or the expression of exposed rooted beliefs and thoughts in the physical reality; thus, both joy and suffering result from it. A man harvests in his life the combination of the sweet and bitter results of the kinds of thoughts and attitudes he more constantly feeds.

A man's thoughts and attitudes determine the way he *feels* and the way he thinks impacts the way he *acts*; finally the way he acts and *responds* to life's challenges will shape his *character* and his *circumstances*. Man's habits will not only build but reveal his character through his circumstances.

Cause and effect is rooted in the hidden area of our thoughts and comes to life in the world of visible and material reality as selfish or unselfish actions.

A noble and God-like character is not a matter of chance. It is the natural result of God touching a man's heart as he reaches out to Him, seeking a personal relationship. As we acknowledge, submit and seek our Creator, God sets free the *desire* and the *ability* within our hearts to continue pursuing the relationship. This gradually translates into right-thinking or God-like thoughts.

Consequently, a noble and God-like character develops and grows in direct proportion to the amount of time we dwell in the presence of God, getting to know His character. This is accomplished through the diligent and persistent study of the Bible as the source of truth, and by seeking His counsel through meditation and prayer.

A man must force and discipline himself into the habit of right, godly thinking. In the initial stages, godly thinking is difficult, but with diligent practice and petition to God for power, it becomes a character-building habit.

In contrast, immoral and uncontrollably corrupt character is developed as a result of man continuing to embrace self-centered, sinister thoughts.

A man is made or destroyed by his own rooted beliefs and thoughts. In the "factory" of his thoughts, he forges the "weapons" by which he destroys himself. However, he can also *choose* to tap into the mind of God, in humility and submission; an act which will lead him to sow and harvest love, joy, strength and peace.

By choosing to submit and to receive God's blessings, a man is *empowered* to redirect the quality of his thoughts. As a result, over the course of his life, this new power will lead him slowly and steadily onto a path toward a Christ-like divine character. Inversely, by the negation and resistance of God and the abuse, neglect and persistent exercise of self-centered thoughts, he will certainly descend, over time, below the level of a beast.

Between these two extremes lie the various grades of character. Man, through his choices and the *quality* of his thoughts and relationship with God, is the architect of his godly habits, character and circumstances.

We are designed with a great capacity to recognize God. Just look around at the beauty and the miracle of nature. But our own individuality, pride and wrong-thinking keep us from relating to God. Sin is a wrong relationship with God — it is not wrong *doing*, but wrong *being*. It is deliberate, determined, persistent and stubborn independence from God, which, as a consequence, triggers rooted personal fears and insecurities.

Man has the freedom to choose his choices, but he cannot choose the consequences of his choices. With each action, God will engineer a consequence for man to experience, according to the lesson of love he must learn. Our personal choices will eventually define our future circumstances through its consequences.

Of all the beautiful Biblical wisdom pertaining to the soul, which have been brought to light through the Word of God, none is more joyful, redemptive, or full of divine promise and confidence than this:

> *A man will never know God personally unless he humbles himself and acknowledges his offenses and*

*self-centeredness. As he turns with a sincere heart from **self** to God through an act of faith, submission and humility, acknowledging his weaknesses and pride, and as he seeks and accepts God's gift of forgiveness for wrong-**being**, he begins a **journey** of reconciliation and love that will transform him and his thoughts into a state of communion with His maker. Then God, using man's thought-life and choices, will give him the power to start molding his character, which in turn will shape his condition, environment, destiny and legacy.*

God will not give men good habits or character and He will not force men to behave correctly before Him. Man must take responsibility for that on his own initiative

A man is not born naturally or supernaturally with character; it must be developed. Although a man is not born with habits, he forms his own habits through his daily thoughts and choices. He is the master of his thoughts and the owner of his choices. A man can either submit to God's calling and make a choice-habit to tap into His Mind to receive the power that he needs to mold godly character within himself, or he can choose to surrender to immoral thoughts, which lead to a path of self-destruction. Either *choice* will eventually become apparent and surface in his reality.

In his natural state, a man is the owner of his own thoughts and choices, holding the key to cultivate every situation in his life. But only through the mind of the Spirit of Christ in a man can he hold within himself that transforming and regenerative activity by which he may change his life and circumstances, as they align with who God *is* and as his thought-life *aligns* with the mind and will of God.

Man is always the master of his thoughts and when he does not seek and ask God for the power to change and transform his life, he is operating under a lower mental state of weakness and depravity, like the foolish master who mishandles his "household."

When he begins to reflect upon his condition, and to search diligently for God to transform his thought-life, he becomes free; a wise conqueror, directing his new inner strength with wisdom and directing his thoughts toward unselfish, worthwhile endeavors.

Only by much searching and digging are gold and diamonds obtained. A man can find the truth connected with God and his being if he will dig deep into the mine of the Truths of God contained in the Bible and understand himself through the eyes of our Creator.

Matthew 7:7 NIV direct us to, ***"...seek and you will find; knock and the door will be opened to you;"*** for only by the practice of meekness, humility, patience, submission to God and constant examination of oneself can a man find his significance based on the love and the wisdom of God. Yes, character building is hard work, but the payoff is a life path of peace and love as we live more closely to and in harmony with God.

A man can accurately search and verify that he is, through his choices, the maker of his character, the architect of his life, and the builder of his destiny, just by watching, controlling, and shifting his thoughts. By carefully scrutinizing even the most trivial past experiences and tracing the effects of each experience upon himself, upon others, and upon his life, he will be able to, time and time again, connect the results of this "cause and effect," "action-reaction" relationship in his circumstances.

THE END RESULT OF THOUGHTS IN YOUR CIRCUMSTANCES

A man's mind may be compared to a garden, intelligently cultivated or allowed to run wild; whether cultivated or neglected, it will *bring forth* a consequence. If no useful seeds are *put* into it, then an abundance of useless weed-seeds will *fall* therein and will continue to produce their kind. Just as a gardener cultivates his garden, keeping it free from weeds and growing the flowers and fruits that he wanted to grow, so could a man watch the garden of his mind to keep "weeds" away. We must continually weed out all the wrong, useless, impure and self-centered thoughts and cultivate toward perfection the flowers and fruits of right, useful, unselfish, pure and godly thoughts.

By pursuing this process of focusing within and understanding who He is, a man sooner or later discovers that, through his thoughts and choices, he *becomes* the master gardener of his soul and the *steward* of his life. He will understand with increasing precision the laws that govern his thoughts and how his thought-process operates in the development of his character, circumstances, and destiny.

Thoughts and character are one; the external conditions of a person's life will always be closely related to his inner condition and to his core beliefs.

This does not mean that a man's circumstance at any given time is an indication of his *entire* character. However, circumstances are so intimately connected with some vital thought-pattern within him that, for the time being, such circumstance is indispensable to his spiritual growth, in order to develop godly character and ultimately learn the path of true unconditional love.

Every man is where he *is* based on who he has *become*. The thoughts that he prevalently cultivates will build into his character, bringing him where he is; in the development of character, there is no element of "luck" or coincidence. This is just as true for those who feel "out of harmony" or discontent with their environment and circumstances as of those who are content with it.

As a progressive and spiritually evolving being, a man is where he is so he may learn to grow in love. As he learns the spiritual lessons contained in every circumstance, it passes away to give place to another set of circumstances, which will cement a new set of lessons of love.

A man is hammered over and over by a particular circumstance so long as he believes himself to be the victim of uncontrollable outside conditions and resistant of learning the lessons contained within. However, when he understands that he has power over the hidden "soil and seeds" of his being, out of which circumstances grow, then he becomes the rightful architect of his own future. He understands why God has engineered that particular circumstance and learns to accept, take ownership, correct, cooperate, and harmonize with the will and purposes of God.

Every time he ventures *out* from his life of faith and allows room for fear, he will be hindered from moving beyond his present circumstances by "logical thinking" instead of relying on his faith to guide him. However, if a man focuses on trusting God, he has no business being concerned about how and where God engineers his circumstances, as he realizes that God is leading his ways in every way, at every moment.

Any man who has for any length of time practiced some discipline knows that circumstances *grow* out of thought. By now, he will have noticed that the change in his circumstances had been in exact proportion with his altered thought-condition and changed attitude.

So true is this that when a man sincerely commits to changing his ways from those things that do not harmonize with who God *is* and decides to *discipline* himself to deal with the defects in his character, he suddenly makes fast and marked change to his outlook in life and spiritual progress. At that point, God permits him to experience a rapid succession of challenges necessary for him to move to the next level of growth and learn the immediate lessons of love and godly character, which are contained within his present circumstance.

The soul attracts that which it secretly hides - that which it treasures, and also that which it fears. *All of our actions in life are motivated either by **love** or **fear**.* Based on this deepest rooted set of beliefs, man's life experience is a combination of both love and fear. The one that he feeds the most is the one that will grow the most.

The only way man can remove fear and reverse a negative thinking process, is to listen to God's assurance. When a man feels helpless he must repeat to himself:

"God is my helper and He is in control at this very moment, even in my present circumstance."

As in nature, every thought-seed planted or allowed to fall into the mind, taking root there, will blossom sooner or later. If fed into a habit, it will bear a similar fruit - good or bad - in our circumstances. Good thoughts and moral choices bear good fruit; bad thoughts bear bad fruit.

Our external circumstances are a reflection of our thought-life. A man does not go to jail by chance, but by the trail of evil thoughts and rooted indiscriminate selfish desires. Nor does a pure-minded man fall suddenly and voluntarily to crime through external forces. For a criminal, the criminal thoughts had long been secretly planted and cultivated in his heart, and the hour of opportunity just revealed its stored inner power.

Therefore, circumstances do not make the man; they are just a reflection of himself and his inner character, revealed by the condition of his heart. A crisis doesn't build something within a man—it simply reveals what he is already made of. Crisis always reveals a man's true character.

No circumstance, such as falling into addictions and its correspondent sufferings, can exist apart from vicious, self-centered, frequently nourished fear-patterns. Neither can a condition of good values and virtue and its resulting joy exist without the continued nurturing of righteous, honorable and god-like aspirations.

In both situations, there is the struggle of man with his own sinful nature, fear, temptation, materialism and selfishness. But man, as the master controller of his choices and thoughts, *in this sense*, is the maker of himself, the shaper and author of his environment.

Men do not attract to their reality that which they *want,* but that which they *are.* If you want to be loved, you have to love first; if you want to be understood, you have to take the time and effort to understand people. If you want godly character, you have to practice the spiritual discipline that will mold you into the image of Jesus. In the same fashion, if you want a great wife, you have to become a great husband...first (or vice-versa).

Our impulses, selfish dreams and ambitions can be spoiled at every step of the way by forces out of our control. But those things that we can control and cannot be spoiled are the moment-by-moment choices we make and the actions we take, which will help us *become* all that we want.

If sin is the ruler in a man's life, God's life in him will gradually be killed. If God is the ruler in man's life, sin in him will gradually diminish. In Luke 17:21 NIV we read, **"The kingdom of God is within you"** –, the purity of God's love is, in fact, in our own very inner self, but so is our natural wretchedness and self-centeredness. Therefore, we must choose who is going to rule our life, God or us.

It is God who works in a man's heart to *will* and to *do* for His own good purpose (Philippians 2:13 NIV).

A man can only control himself. He will not get everything that he wishes or everything he prays for, but God is going to make evident that which he *needs* for his own growth and for the formation of his character. Man's wishes and prayers are only reaffirmed and answered when they harmonize with God's character and conform to who the man *is becoming*. The inner reality of redemption is that God's mind is in constant creation through a man's mind.

In the light of this truth, what then is the meaning of "fighting against circumstances?" It means that a man is continually revolting against an external *effect* - the consequence of his actions - while all the time feeding and preserving its *cause* - the source of the condition - in his heart, thus blocking God's direction.

That condition may take the form of a conscious vice or an unconscious weakness, or inner fear; but whatever it is, it stubbornly delays a man's efforts to change the condition, crying out loud for change through its external circumstances.

It is not until we learn the lesson of overcoming fear through correcting our spiritual belief system and by exercising our conscious and absolute trust in God *(cause)* that we will be in condition to receive the gift of changed circumstances *(effect)*.

I will introduce the following three cases merely as an illustration of the truth that man, through the choosing of good or evil, is the cause, though nearly always unconsciously, of his circumstances:

There is a man who is miserably poor. He is extremely anxious to change his surroundings and home comforts. However, he constantly evades his work, or neglects the *quality* of his work, and considers he is justified in trying to deceive his employer on the ground of the insufficiency of his wages. Such a man does not understand the principles which are the foundation of true prosperity. He is not only totally unfit to rise out of his misery, but is actually attracting to himself a still deeper misery by dwelling in, and acting out, selfish, lazy, deceptive and cowardly thoughts.

There is a rich man who is the victim of a painful and persistent disease as the result of gluttony and not caring for his health. He is willing to give large sums of money to get rid of it, but he will not sacrifice his gluttonous and lustful desires. He wants to indulge his appetite with unhealthy, "junk" foods and have his health as well. Such a man is totally unfit to have good health, because he has defied the natural laws of God and not yet learned the fundamental principles of a healthy life.

There is an employer who adopts deceitful, crooked measures to avoid paying fair wages and, in the hope of making larger profits, reduces the pay of his workforce. Such a man is altogether unfit to prosperity. Then, when he finds himself bankrupt, both as regards to reputation, character and riches, he blames the circumstances, not knowing that he is the sole author of his condition.

A man may be aiming at a good goal, but he is continually frustrating the accomplishment of the goal by encouraging in his mind thoughts and desires which cannot possibly harmonize and are inconsistent with such goal.

Cases like the ones above are plenty and can be illustrated and connected to cause and effect, time and time again. If you are determined, you can trace over a period of time the *activity* of your thought-life with the *results* in your life.

Men are anxious to improve their circumstances, but are unwilling to improve their own character. Therefore, they remain constrained and unsuccessful. However, the man who does not turn away from self-sacrifice and discipline can accomplish the desire of his heart, if it conforms to God's purpose for Him. This is as true of earthly, as well as spiritual matters.

Even the man whose sole objective is to acquire wealth must be prepared to make great personal sacrifices before he can accomplish his goal. How much more so he who desires a strong and well-poised life?

A man may be honest in certain aspects, yet suffer poverty. A man may be dishonest in certain ways, yet acquire wealth. However, the conclusion usually formed that one man fails *because of his particular honesty,* and that the other prospers *because of his particular dishonesty,* is the result of a superficial judgment, which assumes that the dishonest man is almost totally corrupt, and honest man almost entirely virtuous.

In the light of a deeper knowledge and broader experience, such judgment can prove to be erroneous. The dishonest man may have some admirable virtues, which the other does not possess; and the honest man obnoxious vices, which are absent in the other. The honest man reaps the good results of his honest thoughts and acts; however, he also brings upon himself the sufferings that his vices, bad habits and choices produce. Likewise, the dishonest man reaps his own suffering *and* happiness.

Circumstances, however, are so complicated, thought is so deeply rooted, and the conditions of happiness vary so vastly with individuals, that a man's *entire* soul condition cannot be judged by another man from the external aspects of his life alone. Only God can make that judgment, based on His knowledge of a man's heart and motives.

It is pleasing to human vanity and prideful nature to believe that his happiness is exclusively the result of his own virtue. However, a man cannot experience true enduring inner happiness until he experiences harmony with God, so He can *gradually* help eliminate every sickly, bitter, impure and fearful thought from his mind, progressively washing those stains from his soul, which separate and impede him from experiencing the glory and character of God.

Only in this state of mind can he find himself in a condition of humility to be able to recognize and declare that his suffering has been the result of his bad character. That is the point where by a sincere resolution to change his ways, he will place himself in a position of cooperation with God. God cannot change what a man does not acknowledge, confess and repent of.

There is a distinction between God's perfect will and His permissive will, which He uses to accomplish His divine purpose for men's lives. God's perfect will doesn't change. It is with His permissive will and the circumstances that He allows into men's life, that man must struggle before Him. A man doesn't have to fight or wrestle with God, but he must wrestle *before* God with the *cause* of his circumstances.

A man's struggles exist as a result of his own inner opposition between the Spirit of God in him, and his materialistic, selfish nature; between man's desire to do good and his opposite self-centered, sinful, self serving nature.

Through wrestling with temptation, anger, insecurities, fears, impurity, malice, slander and other things that separate a man from God's nature, a man moves himself into a position of recognizing and accepting the supreme realization that he is a sinner, as we all are, saved from his own impure thoughts and self destruction only by the unmerited and unconditional love of God.

At that point, he will find in his mind and life God's Immutable Law, which cannot give good for evil, or evil for good; thus, is absolutely just.

God can only work in a man when he reaches the end of his own rope and in humility, recognizes his human limitations and renounces the desire for controlling things, circumstances and people.

Thus, he must be determined to ask God to take over the control of his life, becoming the architect of the vision God gives him. God, then, becomes the engineer of our circumstances and the master of the outcomes. That is man's point of salvation; and the point of God's regenerative intervention through His Spirit.

Equipped with such a wisdom and awareness, he will then know, looking back upon his past ignorance and blindness, that his life is, and always has been, justly ordered and that all his past experiences, good and bad, were the equitable outworking of his evolving, but not yet fully evolved soul.

Good thoughts and actions can never produce bad results. Bad thoughts and actions can never produce good results. This is but saying that nothing can come from corn but corn, nothing from apples but apples. Men understand this law in the natural world, and work with it. However, few understand it on an emotional, spiritual and moral realm; therefore, we do not cooperate with it.

Suffering is *always* the effect of wrong thinking or doubt in some area. It is an indication that the individual's inner being is out of harmony with God's mind. Disharmony happens when a man is unresponsive to God's gentler guidance and requests.

A man will experience much less internal conflict, fear and suffering if he is convinced that everything that happens in his life works together for good (Romans 8:28 NIV) and that in God's unconditional love, if we ask God for bread, He will not give us a snake instead (Mathews 7:10 NIV).

God uses our *emotion* of suffering to purify, to burn all that is useless and impure in us, in order to strengthen our reliance on Him and to eliminate that which separates man from God. Suffering gradually ceases in those areas where we are becoming pure. As in the gold refining process, there would be no purpose in keep burning the gold after the impurities had been removed.

Sorrow gradually removes man's shallowness, but it does not necessarily always make him better. The only way for man to find himself and develop character in the fire of sorrow, where he can become a blessing for other people, is if he learns his own lessons of love. The Holy Spirit of God continually forces a man to focus his attention inwardly, because each of us has some god-like love qualities, we have not added yet, but must add to our lives.

In the same way, a perfectly pure and ultimately enlightened being through the purifying work of God, such as will be our transformed, glorious heavenly state in the thereafter, could not suffer.

The circumstances which a man encounters with the emotion of suffering are the result of his own mental disharmony with the mind of God. Therefore, in order to liberate himself from all filthiness in his thought-life, he must cooperate with God until he is in harmony with God's nature and character; only then, a man can *experience* God's freedom.

God's blessings, not material possessions, are the measure of right thinking. Misery, not lack of material possessions, is the measure of wrong thinking. A man may be cursed and rich; he may be blessed and poor. Blessedness and riches are only blended together when thought and riches are rightly and wisely used. The poor man only descends into misery when he regards and accepts his fate as a burden unjustly imposed on him.

Indigence and excess are the two extremes of misery. *They are both equally unnatural* and the result of mental chaos. A man is not really fully trained in life until he is a joyful, healthy, and prosperous being. And joy, health, and prosperity are the result of a harmonious adjustment of the inner with the outer, of a man with his surroundings and with God's permissive will and mind with his circumstances. The result of this inner/outer thought-balance is *contentment*.

However, there is an exception to the above rule. Like in the book of Job, God may permit indigence and tragedy to glorify Himself and for His own reasons. God may present a man with circumstances and trials through his lifetime to help him grow stronger, learn the practice of persistence, kill our pride, learn the lessons of love and ultimately, to help others with their own trials. He may do this for a man to be able to understand God's character and mercy and to move a man on with the lessons that will make him grow closer in God's nature and in His love. Man's *attitude* toward God and toward his circumstances, as he goes through trials, will determine the outcome of his internal and external conditions.

A man only begins to be a man when he ceases to whine and revile and commences to search for God's hidden justice, which regulates his life. And as he aligns his mind to God's mind, he ceases to accuse others as the cause of his condition, taking ownership of his *own* condition and building himself up in strong and noble thoughts through the power of God.

If a man indulges in the luxury of encouraging thoughts of misery, he removes God's riches from his life and obstructs others from entering into God's unlimited provision. Self-pity blocks God from a man's life, as he replaces God with his own self-interests and complaints. Self-pity is a state of self- absorption; it is never giving and never satisfied.

A man only begins to be a man when he ceases to kick against circumstances. When he begins to positively *use* them as aids to a more rapid spiritual progress and education, then he discovers the hidden Christ-like potential and possibilities within himself. It is a matter of choosing his own attitude.

Order, not confusion, is the dominating principle in the universe. Justice, not injustice, is the soul and substance of life. And righteousness, not corruption, is the molding and moving force in the spiritual government of the world. This being so, a man finds that life is moral, only when he rights himself with God. During the process of making himself right with God, he will find that as he repents from his past behavior of pride and independence from God and alters his thoughts and attitudes toward situations, things and people, his circumstances involving things and people will start transforming for him.

The proof of this truth is in every person, as it is easily revealed by systematic introspection and self-analysis.

A man's *heart* is his authentic self; it is who he is when he is alone, free of masks and pretensions. Men imagine that thoughts can be kept secret, but they cannot. What is in our hearts rapidly crystallizes into habits, and habits solidify into circumstance.

Let a man radically alter his thoughts and restore and strengthen his relationship with God, and he will be astonished at the rapid transformation it will have in the external conditions of his life.

Degrading thoughts solidify into habits of sensuality and addictions, which solidify into circumstances of destitution and disease. Impure thoughts of every kind crystallize into weakening and confusing habits, which solidify into distracting and adverse circumstances. Thoughts of fear, doubt, and indecision crystallize into weak, insecure and irresolute habits, which solidify into circumstances of failure, indigence, and slavish dependence.

Lazy thoughts crystallize into habits of uncleanness and dishonesty, which solidify into circumstances of filth and beggary. Hateful, judgmental and condemnatory thoughts crystallize into habits of accusation, pride and violence, which solidify into circumstances of harm, paranoia and persecution. Selfish thoughts of all kinds crystallize into habits of self-seeking, which solidify into stressful circumstances.

> *"To the pure, all things are pure, but to those who are corrupted and do not believe, nothing is pure. In fact, both their minds and consciences are corrupted" (Titus 1:15 NIV)*
>
> Jesus said, *"For out of the heart come evil thoughts, murder, adultery, sexual immorality, theft, false testimony, slander" (Matthew 15:19-20 NIV).*

On the other hand, pure, beautiful godly thoughts of all kind crystallize into habits of grace and kindliness, which solidify into affable, unselfish and cheerful circumstances. Pure thoughts crystallize into habits of temperance and self-control, which solidify into circumstances of rest and peace. Thoughts of courage, self-reliance, and decision crystallize into self-controlled habits, which solidify into circumstances of success, and plenty, *with freedom.*

Energetic thoughts crystallize into habits of cleanliness and industry, which solidify into circumstances of love. Gentle and forgiving thoughts crystallize into habits of gentleness, which solidify into protective circumstances. Loving and unselfish thoughts crystallize into habits of forgiveness toward others, which solidify into circumstances of sure and abiding prosperity and true riches

> *"All the ways of the Lord are loving and faithful to those who keep the demands of his covenant" (Psalms 25:10 NIV).*
>
> *"For I know the plans I have for you," declares the LORD, "plans to prosper you and not to harm you, plans to give you hope and a future" (Jeremiah 29:11 NIV).*

A particularly persistent train of thought, whether it is good or bad, cannot fail to produce its fruit on our character and circumstances. A man cannot *directly* choose his circumstances - only God can do that - but he can choose his thoughts; and so indirectly, yet surely, God will shape and adjust his circumstances accordingly. If man's dreams conform to God's character, God helps him realize his dreams.

What a man mostly encourages will be presented in opportunities, which will most speedily bring to the surface both man's good and evil thoughts. This is a test of wills and a man's point of choice between God's will and His thoughts, and a man's desires to control and compete with God through imposing his own will.

Let a man cease from his sinful thoughts and negative attitudes, and the entire world will soften toward him and be ready to help him. Let him put away his weak and sickly thoughts, attitudes and fears and lo!...opportunities will spring up on every front to aid his strong determination. Let him encourage good thoughts and *accept* God's forgiveness and his future will not bind him down to wretchedness and shame.

Man's Thoughts and Crisis

The circumstances a man is going through are either making him sweeter, better and nobler, or they are making him more critical, fault-finding, and insistent on his own way. A man's circumstances either make him bitter and evil, or they make him more righteous, depending entirely on his relationship with God, his level of intimacy with Him, and his attitude.

A man's character determines how he interprets the will of God. If he stays true to God, He will take him through trials that will serve to bring a man into a better knowledge of God and himself.

Sometimes God sends a man through a crisis in private, where no other person can help him. After he has persevered through the fires of life in total submission and trust in God, slowly but surely there will be nothing much that will be able to bother or depress him, unless he changes his focus back from God to his own *self*.

This is clearly illustrated in Proverb 3:5-7 NIV: ***"Trust in the LORD with all your heart and lean not on your own understanding; in all your ways acknowledge him, and he will make your paths straight"***. ***Do not be wise in your own eyes; reverence the LORD and turn away from evil."***

A man must make a determination to go on through the crisis, submitting all that he *has* and all that he *is* to God. God will then equip him to do all that He requires of him and will make His paths known, so he can firmly walk in them.

A man should never be afraid when God brings back his past. He must let his memory have its way with him, as it may be a reminder from God bringing its rebuke and sorrow in order to make a man aware of areas he must change in order to learn true love. God will turn painful, shameful thoughts into a wonderful lesson of growth for the future, if a man remains open to God's gentle warnings and guidance. God also often reminds a man of his past to protect him from a very shallow security in the present.

If a man fails to learn the lessons brought to him through his circumstances, it is because he has not yet put into practice the lesson's God placed within him. A crisis will reveal whether or not he has been putting God's lessons of love into practice.

The clouds of sorrows, sufferings, or providential circumstances teach us how to walk by faith, trusting God with all our heart. If there were no clouds in our lives, we would have no faith or hope. Furthermore, every cloud God permits our way is designed to *unlearn* something.

Sometimes God will take a man through a number of experiences that are not meant for him personally at all. They are designed to enable him to understand what takes place in the lives of others, in order to help him grow in compassion and love, giving him an opportunity to intercede for them.

God may not will another person to sin against you. Nevertheless, He may will that the results or the outcome of being sinned against will be for His glory and the result for you will be improved patience, forgiveness and compassion.

In the same way, you may sin against another and the destruction and pain that it works in you will be for your good and for your spiritual development.

As crises arise, as they most certainly will, a man should not faint and give up, but seek after the reason, increase the intensity of his search and examine the evidence which brought him there in the first place. Then he can reverse the course of events by dealing with the cause, rather than wrestling with the effects.

THE IMPACT OF THOUGHTS ON YOUR HEALTH AND BODY

The body is the servant of the mind. It obeys the functions of the mind. The body sinks rapidly into disease and decay, responding to dishonest or impure thoughts; in the same way, joyful and beautiful thoughts transform the body with youthfulness and beauty.

Disease and health, like circumstances, originate and are rooted in thought. Sickly thoughts will manifest themselves through a sickly body. Thoughts of fear have been known to kill a man as speedily as a bullet, and they are continually killing thousands of people just as surely, although less quickly. The people who live in fear of disease are the people who get it. When a man lives in constant fear of becoming sick, he will gradually make himself sick through the stress caused by anxiety and the power of his own thoughts.

Anxiety and stress quickly weaken the body's immune system and lay it open to the entrance of disease, while impure thoughts, even if the body is not indulged, will soon shatter the nervous system.

As a point of clarification: pure thoughts will not cure an already sickened body worn out by years of worry, fear, abuse, evil and secretly fostered impure thoughts. Strong, pure, cheerful and peaceful thoughts build up the body and keep it strong in energy and grace, but thoughts alone will not cure years of abusive thinking and poor habits.

God may choose to work his healing mercies through medical doctors, using them as His instrument of healing; or He can decide to directly intervene through miraculous healing. However, a man remains responsible for changing his indulgent habits and thoughts, through his submission to the power of God, if he is to remain healthy.

Strong, pure, cheerful and peaceful thoughts build up the immune system and increase its energy. The body is a delicate instrument, which responds voluntarily to the thoughts by which it is fed, and habits of thought will produce their own effects, good or bad, upon it. *An anxious heart weighs a man down, but a kind word cheers him up" (Proverbs 12:25).*

A man will continue to have impure and poisoned blood so long as he disseminates and stimulates unclean thoughts. Out of a clean thought-life comes a clean life and a clean, healthy body.

Out of a corrupted, self-centered mind proceed a corrupted life and a corrupted body. Thought is the source of action, life and manifestation; make the source cleaner, and your body will be healthier.

Change of a diet will not help a man who will not change his thoughts. After a man changes his thought-life through submission to God, he no longer desires "junk" or unhealthy food.

If you want to perfect your body, guard your mind and change your unhealthy eating and exercising habits. If you want to renew your body, beautify your mind by filling it with Christ-like thoughts of unconditional love.

Thoughts of malice, envy, disappointment and despondency rob the body of its health and grace. *"A heart at peace gives life to the body"* (Proverbs 14:30 NIV). A sour face does not come by chance; it is made by sour thoughts. Wrinkles marked by bitterness are drawn by recklessness, uncontrolled passion and unchecked pride.

I once heard about a woman of ninety-six who had the bright, innocent face of a girl. I heard about a man well under middle age whose face was drawn into an inharmonious anger-looking semblance.

The first is the result of a sweet and cheerful attitude; the other is the outcome of misguided passion, disharmonious and discontent with life.

As you cannot have a fresh and healthy house unless you let fresh air and sunshine flow freely into its rooms, so a strong body and a cheerful, joyful or serene attitude can only be attained from the free access of the light of God into your mind. Those light-thoughts produce in the outer world *love, joy, peace, patience, kindness, goodness, faithfulness, gentleness and self-control* (Galatians 5:22 NIV).

On the faces of the aged, there are wrinkles made by kindness; others are made by strong and pure thoughts and still others are sculpted by obsessions. Who cannot distinguish them?

For those who have lived righteously, age is calm, peaceful, and softly mellowed, like the setting sun. I know about a man, whose pursuit in life was to seek godly wisdom. On his deathbed, he was not aged except in years. He died as sweetly and peacefully as he had lived.

There is no medicine like a cheerful thought for lessening the ills of the body. There is no reliever that compares with kindness to eradicate the shadows of grief and sorrow.

Choosing to live continually in thoughts of fear, cynicism, suspicion, and envy is to be confined to a self-made prison. However, choosing to think well of all, to be joyful with all, to patiently learn to find the good in all - such unselfish thoughts are the very gates of heaven. To choose to dwell day by day in thoughts of love toward every creature will bring abundant peace to your reality.

> *"We wait in hope for the LORD; he is our help and our shield. In him our hearts rejoice, for we trust in his holy name. May your unfailing love rest upon us, O LORD, even as we put our hope in you" (Psalms 33:20 – 22).*

Thought, Purpose and Determination

Until thought is linked with godly focus and purpose, there is no intelligent accomplishment. The majority of people allow their "ship of thought" to "drift" upon the ocean of life. Lack of purpose and focus is a vice and a weakness, and such drifting must not continue for those who choose to steer clear of catastrophe and destruction.

Joy comes from experiencing the complete fulfillment of the specific purpose God has for us and for which man was created. It does not come from successfully doing something of a man's own choosing without a godly purpose. A man's purpose in life is to submit, seek and love God and to love his fellow humans, out of an inner gratitude for the goodness and the love of God in his life.

Those who have no central godly purpose at the center of their life fall an easy prey to worry, fear, trouble, and self-pity, all of which are indicative of weakness. They lead, just as surely as deliberately planned sins although by a different route, to failure, unhappiness, and loss, for weakness cannot persist in a God-centered world. Light and darkness cannot dwell in the same house.

After praying to God for direction and wisdom, a man should seek and visualize the specific purpose placed by God in his heart and set out to accomplish it using the talents and gifts God has equipped him with. He should make this purpose and vision the central point of his thoughts.

All unselfish, creative ideas come from God. Ideas may take the form of a spiritual ideal, or it may be a worldly object; but a godly purpose must always include the love for God and service to our fellow humans as the center of man's *motive*.

Whatever a man's purpose or destiny is, he should steadily focus his thought-forces upon God's will over the specific purpose, vision, or destiny which God has set before him.

God engineers a man's circumstances in order to take him to a place where He can prepare that man to fulfill God's planted vision and purpose in life.

A man should make the pursuing of God's specific purpose for him his supreme duty and should devote himself to its attainment, not allowing his thoughts to wander away into short-lived fantasies, longings, and worthless thoughts. This is the majestic road to self-control, discipline and true concentration of thought. Even if he fails repeatedly to accomplish his purpose - as he necessarily must until weakness is overcome - the strength of godly character gained will be the measure of his *true* success, triggering a new starting point or launching pad for future spiritual and personal inner power and triumph.

Those who God has not *yet* prepared for the uneasiness of a great *legacy* should focus their thoughts in the present upon flawlessly performing their current responsibilities, no matter how insignificant their present assignment may appear.

Current assignments serve to gather and focus our thoughts, strengthen our determination and develop inner strength and future power. If this is done, there is nothing which cannot be accomplished: **"*I can do everything through Him who gives me strength*"** (Philippians 4:13 NIV).

Even the weakest individual will be transformed if he believes this truth: *that strength can only be developed by struggle, effort, perseverance and practice*. Once this is applied and effort is added to effort, patience to patience, and strength to strength, never giving up, that man will at last grow divinely *strong*.

As a physically weak man can make himself strong by carefully and patiently building muscle through strength-training workouts, so the man of weak thoughts can make them strong by exercising the habit of patient, moment-by-moment submission to God in order to experience His Spirit and to develop the power of right thinking.

Choosing to reject lack of direction and weakness, and choosing to begin concentrating on thinking with a divine purpose, is to enter the ranks of those strong ones who only recognize failure as one of the pathways to accomplishment; who make all conditions serve them, and who think strongly, attempt fearlessly, and accomplish masterfully. It is only in that state of mind and attitude that God can reveal His personal legacy to a man.

If a man does not apply God's revealed vision to the issues of everyday life, the vision will never be fulfilled. It is at the expense of a man's well-being if he chooses to get caught up in practical *self-serving* busy-work, only to miss the fulfillment of his appointed vision and legacy.

Having envisioned God's purpose and legacy for his own life, a man should sit and plan a *straight* pathway to its achievement, looking neither to the right nor to the left.

Doubts and fears should be rigorously excluded by totally trusting God, for where God *Is*, there is no fear or doubt. Fear and doubt are disintegrating elements, which break up the straight line of effort, rendering it crooked, ineffectual, and useless. Thoughts of doubt and fear will never accomplish anything; they always lead to failure.

When a man ceases to trust God's purpose, man's strength, initiative, energy, and positive-thinking cease and doubt and fear creep in.

The will to do springs from the awareness that we *can* do - **"I can do everything through Him who gives me strength" (Phil 4:13 NIV).** Doubt and fear are the great enemies of knowledge and wisdom, and he who encourages them, who does not exterminate them by living in total submission to God, defeats himself at every step.

He who has conquered doubt and fear has conquered failure. If man's every thought is aligned with the power of God, all difficulties are bravely met and wisely overcome. Under this state of grace, God favorably plants His purposes and they bloom and bring forth fruit, which does not fall prematurely to the ground. ***"For God did not give us a spirit of timidity, but a spirit of power, of love and of self-discipline"*** *(*2 Tim 1:7 NIV).

Thought applied fearlessly and with determination toward a goal becomes a powerful creative and effective force. He who *understands* this concept is ready to become something higher and stronger than a mere bundle of wavering thoughts and fluctuating feelings. He who *does* this, has become the conscious and intelligent master of his God-given mental powers, as we are created in the image of God and are designed to operate *through* the power of God - ***"Let us make man in our image, in our likeness"*** *(*Genesis 1:26 NIV).

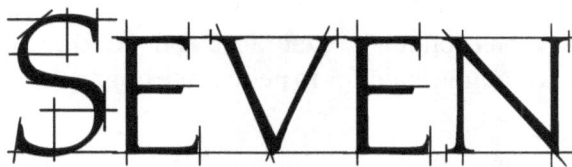

THOUGHTS AND ACHIEVEMENT

All that a man achieves and all that he fails to achieve is the direct result of the quality of his own thoughts, beliefs, and rooted assumptions. In a justly ordered creation, where loss of equilibrium would mean total destruction, individual and personal responsibility must be absolute.

A man's weakness and strength, purity and impurity, are his own, not another man's. They are brought about by himself, and not by another; and they can only be altered by himself, not by another. His condition is his own, not another man's. His suffering and his happiness evolved from within himself, based on the quality of his character. *As he thinks, so he is*; as he continues to think, *so he remains*.

A strong man cannot help a weaker man, unless the weaker is *willing* to be helped, and even then the weak man must become strong within himself. He must, in God's power, but by his own resolution, develop the strength which he admires in another. None but himself can alter his chosen mental condition.

It has been common for men to think, *"Many men are slaves because one is an oppressor; let us hate the oppressor."* However, there is also a tendency to reverse this judgment, and to say, *"One man is an oppressor because many are slaves; let us despise the slaves."* The truth is that master and slave are co-operators in ignorance and fear. While it seems they are both afflicting each other, in reality, they are, afflicting themselves to fulfill each other's hidden perverse agenda and secret motives. Conventional wisdom attributes the exploitation of the slave to the weakness of the oppressed and the misapplied power of the oppressor. However, perfect love, seeing the suffering which both parties cause out of ignorance, condemns neither. Perfect love and compassion embrace both oppressor and oppressed.

He who has conquered ignorance and weakness by diligently controlling his thoughts belongs to neither the oppressor or oppressed. *He is free.*

A man can only rise, conquer, and achieve a goal *with peace of mind* by restoring and pursuing his relationship with God and lifting up his thoughts and strength to Him. He can only remain weak, hopeless and miserable by refusing to submit and align his thoughts with God, choosing instead to struggle by living independently from his Creator.

Before a man can achieve anything, even in worldly pursuits, he must lift his thoughts above over-indulgence and selfishness. This doesn't mean that man may not, in order to succeed, give up *all* cruelty and selfishness, but at least a portion of it must be surrendered to achieve some degree of success.

A man is not created, by design, to stand alone from God and act independently; therefore, he must be careful to choose godly and unselfish thoughts more readily than selfish, fear- and sin-based thoughts.

A man whose most prevalent thoughts are polluted with self-indulgence could neither think clearly nor plan methodically. He could not find and develop his inner resources, and would fail in any undertaking. By not controlling his thoughts, he would not be in a position to have power over serious affairs and to adopt serious responsibilities. A man's potential is only limited by the thoughts that he chooses.

A man's success in this world will be in the measure that he surrenders his confused, carnal, materialistic thoughts and depends on God for the development of his plans and the strengthening of his determination.

Determination, combined with faith - trust in God - is what keeps us going when circumstances contradict our God-given vision.

The higher a man lifts his thoughts and character to God, the more godly, upright, and righteous he becomes, the greater his *true success* (without pain) will be, and the more blessed and enduring will be his achievements and legacy. ***"Do not be conformed to this world, but be transformed by the renewing of your mind, that you may prove what is good and acceptable and perfect will of God"*** (Rom 12:2 NIV).

The world does not favor the greedy, the dishonest, or the vicious, although on the mere surface it may sometimes appear to do so. The world respects the honest, the generous, and the righteous. All the great teachers of the ages have declared this in different ways, and to prove and *recognize* it, a man just has to persist in pursuing Christ-like character through continuously lifting up his thoughts to God.

Intellectual achievements are the result of thought committed to the search for knowledge, or for the beauty and truth in life and nature. Such achievements may be sometimes connected with vanity and ambition, but this is not normally the case. For the most part, those achievements are the natural result of long and arduous effort and of pure and unselfish thinking.

Spiritual achievements are the consummation of holy aspirations as we respond and submit through the unmerited gift of grace through God's call.

He who lives constantly desiring, seeking and pursuing godly, righteous, moral and elevated thoughts abides in God. By choosing all that is compassionate and unselfish, he will, as surely as the sun rises and sets, become wise, a noble man of godly character. Only then, he will be able to rise into a position of positive influence and blessing to others, which will become his reward.

Achievement of any kind is the reward of effort, the crown of thought. Assisted by self-discipline, resolution, purity, righteous character and well-directed thought, a man ascends. By the aid of wretchedness, indolence, impurity, corruption and confusion of thought, a man descends.

A man may rise to high success in the world, and even to great maturity in the spiritual realm, and again descend into weakness and wretchedness by *allowing* prideful, arrogant, selfish, and corrupt sinful thoughts to take possession of him.

Victories attained by right thought can only be maintained by vigilance and the power of *prayer* and submission to God. Many give in when success is assured and rapidly fall back into failure.

All achievements, whether in the business, intellectual, or spiritual worlds, are the result of specifically directed thoughts and sacrifices.

He who would accomplish little must sacrifice little. If a person is ever going to do anything worthwhile, there will be times when he must risk everything and go out on a limb, trusting God with all his heart for the outcome.

He who would achieve much must sacrifice much. He who would reach highly must sacrifice greatly. There can be no progress, no achievement, without sacrifice.

All *worthy* achievements, whether in the business, intellectual, or spiritual world (whether we are conscious or not) are gifts from God, received through man's personal relationship with his Creator, and powerfully released and directed by disciplined thought and a submissive attitude.

> *"Finally, brothers, whatever is true, whatever is noble, whatever is right, whatever is pure, whatever is lovely, whatever is admirable-- if anything is excellent or praiseworthy—think about those things"* (Philippians 4:8 NIV).

VISIONARY DREAMS

The dreamers are the developers of the world. As the invisible world, the spiritual realm, becomes visible in the material world through the dreamer's dreams, so men are inspired by the beautiful visions of their solitary dreamers. Humanity cannot forget its dreamers. It cannot let their ideals fade and die. They live in them. It knows them in the *realities,* which it shall one day see and experience.

Composer, architect, sculptor, theologian, painter, poet, entrepreneur, scholars; these are the makers of the world, the architects of dreamland. They are God's instruments and pamphleteers. The world is more beautiful because they have lived, dared to dream big dreams and were willing to pay the price to make them come true. Without them, laboring humanity would perish. He who cherishes a beautiful vision, a lofty ideal in his heart, will one day see it through. Beautiful dreams and visions are God's way of self expression through men in the material realm.

Columbus cherished a vision of another world, and he discovered it. Copernicus fostered the vision of a multiplicity of worlds and a wider universe, and he revealed it. God, through Jesus the Christ, beheld His vision of saving humanity through His incarnation in Jesus, as He revealed to humanity His plan of a spiritual world of stainless beauty and perfect peace, love and oneness with Him; He fulfilled it. Through God's vision and Jesus' awareness of His mission on earth, He died for us, giving us forgiveness of sins and restoring the Way to enter a personal relationship of love with God.

Treasure your dreams. Treasure your ideals. Treasure the music that stirs in your heart, the beauty that God forms in your mind, and the loveliness that clothes your purest thoughts, for out of them will grow all delightful conditions, all heavenly environments. If you but remain true to your vision, trusting God in *every* circumstance, your world will, at last, be built, and joy and peace will be yours.

Dream big dreams, and as you dream, seek God for His vision; as you dream, so shall you become. Your vision is the promise of what you shall one day be. Your ideal and revealed sense of legacy is the foresight of what you can at last achieve through perseverance.

The greatest achievements were at first and for a time a dream. The oak sleeps in the acorn; the bird waits in the egg; and in the highest vision of the soul, God *Is*. Dreams are the seeds of future realities.

As you dream big, noble dreams, you must always live with a constant reminder that you must never define yourself through material success because you can lose your head to pride.

Even if your current circumstances are unpleasant, they shall not long remain so if you identify God's purpose for your life and strive to reach it. You cannot travel *within* and stand still *without*.

I know about a young man hard pressed by poverty and labor, confined long hours in an unhealthy workplace. He was unschooled, and lacking all the arts of refinement. But he dreamed of better things. His thoughts were of intelligence, of refinement, of grace and beauty. He trusted God, prayed, visualized his God-given inspiration (*"in-*[God's] *spirit"*), and mentally created an ideal condition of life - God's purpose and legacy for him.

The vision of a wider freedom and a larger scope took possession of him. The Holy Spirit allowed him to feel unrest, which urged him to action. He began to utilize all of his spare time and means, small though they were, to the relentless development of godly character and needed resources to pursue his God-given purpose, vision and legacy.

Very soon so altered had his mind become that the workplace could no longer hold him. His mentality became so disharmonious with his environment that his present situation fell out of his life, as a garment is set aside. With the increased new opportunities, which fitted the extent of his expanding faculties, he moved out of his present circumstances forever.

Years later, we see this youth as a full-grown man. We find him a master of certain Biblical principles involving the expansion, discipline, unselfishness and dominion of his mind, which he exercises with worldwide influence and almost unequaled power. In his hands he holds gigantic responsibilities and positive leadership assignments by divine appointment. He speaks, and lives are changed. He becomes an instrument appointed by God, around which innumerable men are inspired and destinies change and evolve. He has realized the vision of his youth. He has *become* one with his ideal and with his God-given vision and legacy.

If your hopes and dreams seem to be experiencing disappointment and frustration right now, it may simply mean that they are being purified. Every hope and dream of the human mind can be fulfilled, provided that our motives are noble and of God and that a man perseveres in its attainment.

Perseverance means more than staying power — more than simply holding on until the end. Faith is not a weak and pious emotion but a strong and dynamic *confidence* built on the *conviction* of the fact that God is holy love, is in control of *everything* and *truly* cares for each one of us.

And even though you may not see God right now and cannot understand what He is doing, you *must* trust Him *completely*. Trusting God for His deliverance must be the supreme effort of your life. The real meaning of eternal life here and now is a life that can face anything it has to face without hesitation, because you trust God completely.

And you, too, my beloved reader, will realize the vision (not the wishful thinking) of your heart, for you will always gravitate toward that which you secretly love and have a passion for.

The responsibility of the exact results of your own thoughts will be placed into your hands. You will receive that which you *earn*; no more, no less. Whatever your present environment may be, you will fall, remain, or rise with your thoughts, your vision, God's ideal for you. You will become as small as your controlling desire; as great as your dominant and highest aspiration, godly thoughts and your developed character.

The thoughtless, the ignorant, and the lazy, seeing only the *apparent* effects of things and not the things themselves, talk of luck, fortune, and chance. Seeing a man grow rich, they say, "How lucky he is!" Observing another become wise, they exclaim, "How highly privileged he is!"

And noting the godly character and positive influence and leadership of another, they remark, "How 'luck' aids him every time!"

They do not see the trials, failures and struggles which these men have voluntarily encountered in order to gain strength and faith and while pursuing godly wisdom. They have no knowledge of the sacrifices they have made, of the undaunted efforts they have put forth, of the faith they have exercised, that they might overcome the "impossible" to realize the vision God placed in their hearts. They do not know the darkness and the heartaches of wrestling with fear; they only see the light and joy. They call it "luck," for they do not see the long and arduous journey, but only behold the pleasant goal. They do not understand the process, but only perceive the visible results and call it "chance."

In all human affairs there are *efforts,* and there are *results,* and the strength of the effort is the measure of the result - chance is not. The development of man's spiritual gifts, positive power, and material, intellectual, and spiritual possessions are the fruits of effort and trust in God. They are thoughts fulfilled, goals accomplished, visions realized.

The vision that you exalt in your mind, the ideal that you set apart in your heart, the knowledge and wisdom you gain about who

God is and who you are as His child - this you will build your life around and this your character will become.

The Inner Silence and Submission to God!

When a man makes a commitment to experience God in humility and submission, his life starts a path of ascension to a higher level of spiritual growth.

The key to any good human relationship is communication. The more frequent and the deeper the communication, the better we are going to get to know a person. The key to getting to know God, His purposes, His will and His love is also communication.

There are various ways to communicate with God. One is silence of *words*, *thoughts*, and of *desires*. The silence of words is when we silence our inner talk and shut down our reason and judgments. The silence of thoughts is when we go inside to the center of our beings where Christ dwells and we sit in His presence just to *experience* Him and to wait for His teaching. The third silence is the silence of desires where we do not ask for anything but only desire to *love Him*

After experiencing God, volunteer to obey Him without doubt or fear. Do not act if there is fear, as fear does not come from God. True obedience to God is selfless; it has no personal interest of gain for oneself. Obedience is about following God's instructions and not about us, and what we can gain.

As the inner man starts growing stronger than our natural man through humility, submission, obedience and the seeking and experiencing of God, a clear fountain of love for God arises and increases, allowing a man to receive deeper understanding of God and His ways.

Although the lessons will come in different ways, the ultimate purpose of all lessons is to glorify God by dying to our *self* so that our only desire becomes to fulfill His will on earth - to worship and love Him and through the overflow of His love, to love our neighbor.

The test of knowing if you are fully resigned to the will of God is when you are not troubled anymore of other people's opinion about you. When we make other people's opinions about ourselves override God's approval and opinion about us, then we have made other people's opinion a little idol in our lives.

We cannot be hurt by men. We cannot be hurt by devils. We can only be hurt by our own self and pride and the ferocity of our pride and desires. The greatest devil of all is our own pride and our *self*.

The Inner Calm

Peace of mind is one of the beautiful jewels of wisdom, *a gift* enjoyed by man resulting from a harmonious relationship with his Creator. It is the result of long and patient choices in self-discipline focused on God, as a man's mind synchronizes with God's character. God's presence, evidenced by serenity, is an indication of mature experience, a greater-than-ordinary knowledge of who God is and a mastery of the right use of thought.

A man becomes calm inside to the degree that he understands himself as a thought-evolved child of God. As he develops a clearer understanding of the laws of cause and effect, sin and consequence, he ceases to fuss, fume, worry and grieve, and God gives him the power to remain poised, steadfast and serene.

A man with inner calm, having learned how to govern himself, knows how to adapt himself to others; and others, in turn, admire his spiritual strength, which comes from the inner Christ within. They feel that they can learn from him and rely on him.

The more tranquil a man becomes, the greater is his success, his influence, and his power for good.

Even an ordinary businessman will find that his prosperity

increases as he develops greater self-control and equanimity. People will always prefer to deal with a man whose demeanor is strongly and steadily composed.

The strong, calm man is always loved and revered. He is like a shade-giving tree in a thirsty land, or a sheltering rock in a storm. Who does not love a person with a tranquil heart and a sweet-tempered, balanced life?

It does not matter whether it rains or shines, or what changes come to those possessing these blessings, for they are always lovable, serene, and calm. That exquisite poise of character, which we call serenity, is the result of lessons from God, learned; it is the blossoming of life, the harvest of the soul. It is as precious as wisdom, more to be desired than gold; yes, than even fine gold.

Money-seeking people look insignificant in comparison to those with a serene life; a life that dwells in the ocean of truth, beneath the waves, beyond the reach of tempests, in the eternal calm…where God *Is*!

How many people we know who sour their lives, who ruin all that is sweet and beautiful with explosive tempers, who destroy their poise of character, and cause bad blood! It is without question that the great majority of people ruin their lives and spoil their happiness by lack of self-control. How few people we meet in life who are well-balanced, who have that exquisite poise which is characteristic of a mature, godly character!

Yes, humanity burns with uncontrolled passion, is confused with ungoverned grief and driven about by anxiety, fear and doubt. Only a wise man, whose thoughts are controlled and cleansed, make the winds and the storms of the soul obey him, as the wind obeyed Jesus in Mark 4:39-41, when He rebuked the wind and said to the sea, **"*Peace, be still and the wind ceased and there were a great calm*"** (Mark 4:39).

Disturbed souls, wherever you are and in whatever conditions you may live under, know this: In the ocean of life, there is an island where God is waiting for you, smiling, ready to love you. He awaits your coming. Keep your hand firmly upon the control of your thoughts. That island is in the core of your soul; it is where the Spirit of God lies. He is on call, ready to help.

Reach out to Him and ask for help. Faith - trusting God in *every* circumstance - *is life*; self-discipline is strength; right thought is mastery; inner calm is power.

Choose God; Choose life; and say unto your heart right now, ***"Peace, be still and know that God is in you!"***

PROLOGUE

LIFE APPLICATION AND ACTION POINTS

1. If you have asked yourself, "Is this all there is in life?" you may be at the point where you are starting to take a serious look at the things in life that really matter. The first matter to realize is that God loves you so much to the point of coming to earth in history, incarnating in Jesus and dying to restore your relationship with Him to make you realize His unconditional love. Just imagine, the Creator of the universe is your loving father! That makes you co-creator as His son/daughter. Make a life-changing decision to acknowledge (you can't change what you don't acknowledge) that you have made many less-than-righteous mistakes in the past and need to be forgiven; ask Him for forgiveness, and as *your Father* He will. Ask Him to take control of your life and to work His love through you and to guide you through the maze of life; He will. Finally, *believe* (trust Him with all of your heart) that what you asked will be done, and most importantly, forgive *yourself* from all your past transgressions, as God Himself has already done for you. Then, get ready to start a brand new and magnificent life in communion with God. Your life will be in the path of a total transformation. Your life will not be trouble-free, but you will start to *realize* your purpose in life, which will change your outlook and attitudes in life. God will change the way you respond to *any* circumstance.

2. Make a conscious choice to meditate in God's Word by reading one chapter of the Bible every morning, before engaging in your daily work. Just wake up half an hour earlier to talk with God. At the end of the year, you will find that you will spend 182 hours getting to know yourself through God and getting to know the beauty and the character of God. After practicing this for 30 days it will become the healthiest, most life-transforming *habit* of your life.

3. As you encounter life's challenges (as you certainly will), remember that God, the Creator of the universe, *your father*, is in control of everything. If you believe that God loves you, and that He will never send any circumstance your way to harm you, peace will overtake you. As you get to know Him, you will develop the *conviction* that this is true all of the time and in every circumstance. As you see Him *always* working for your good, you will develop a *trust* in God and a bond of love, like no other relationship will ever offer you.

4. In every circumstance, just remind yourself that there is a lesson of love especially designed for you to grow. Every circumstance is an opportunity to grow and to develop the actions of love.

5. The older and wiser you become, the more you will realize that *most of the things that you see are not what they appear to be*. The material world is a world of pretension, deception and illusions. Make the habit to postpone judgment on things, people and circumstances until you have had the opportunity to truly see beyond the appearances and gather the facts.

6. When you find yourself having materialistic, sensual, immoral, fearful thoughts (as you will from time to time), choose to switch your thoughts by affirming the contrary. Immediately ask God to give you the *power* to choose and evolve the quality of your thoughts. You will be surprised how quickly you will be able to control your thoughts, if you just try to trust God.

7. Your mind and your body are connected. Make a habit to nourish your body with healthy foods, exercise regularly and seek peace through a personal relationship with God. *Worries are negative goal-setting; it is thinking and dwelling on those things that you don't want to happen. Trust God totally and completely to bring provision and healing in your relationships, emotions and physical body.*

8. Love comes as a consequence of our interpretation and realization of who God is, His love for us, our love for Him and who we are as His children. Fear comes as a man takes his

eyes off God and focuses on the interpretation of the events and circumstances in his life based on, and influenced by, past experiences and beliefs, instead of trusting God.

9. Set very specific goals for your life based on those things you feel more passionate about and the specific gifts that God has given you. Make specific plans on how to achieve those goals and set a date when you are going to start working on those goals and when you plan to finish. Break them down in monthly tasks for attainment. Most importantly, act your plan.

10. Surrender the control of your life to God daily, in the morning, noon and in the evening. Just talk to God and tell Him sincerely, **"Lord, you are in control of everything. I am surrendering my circumstances and my life to you right now."** You will see what an amazing difference this act of faith and trust will make in your life!

Works Cited

Barrs, Dr. Jerome. To Be Human. (Out of Print).

Holy Bible: New International Version. Grand Rapids: Zondervan, 1978.

Lewis, C.S., Mere Christianity

Reimann, James, eds. Streams in the Desert: 366 Daily Devotional Readings. Rev. Ed. Grand Rapids: Zondervan, 1997. Print

Testimonials

Forbes Book Reviews:

★★★★★

Excellent book with great information that is written in a concise manner that requires the reader to think. It could change your life in the most positive way.

amazon.com Book Reviews:

★★★★★ **Renew your mind!,**

This book takes no time to get down to the nitty-gritty and changes your perspective on circumstance. Our thought life really is more significant than we make it out to be and we ought to be more aware of its out-pouring into our daily lives.

Candido's sincerity in this book proposes a certain clarity that is difficult to find in other philosophical and theological publications. Although it is a short read it offers a lot to chew on. I recommend reading it a number of times- M. LANGHOFF

It is often said that Dynamite comes in small packages. This is an example that makes the "cliché". An articulate weaving of spiritual and practical knowledge. In fact, you learn, if you didn't know already, that the spiritual truth of God is the most practical of all. If you already knew, you are reinforced and motivated to action in any endeavor in which you are involved. Segarra's writing will increase clarity, confidence and purpose in your life; all in a very quick read that you will enjoy and want to read over and over- S. BREED

★★★★★ **Must Read!**

This book is very instructive on how we all are accountable for our destiny and how we can improve our relationship with our God by applying the Bible's principles and taking ownership for our acts

and thoughts. -R. DELGADO

★★★★★ Outstanding reading!!

This book really was thought-provoking! It brought to the surface many issues I hadn't thought deeply about. I had to read it twice! I am already seeing life in a different way! It's worth your time...read it! -C. LEAR

★★★★★ Essential to your thought life!!!

This book provides an in depth look at your quality of thought and how it affects the outcome of your life. It is a quick read that contains the keys to unlocking your potential. This is one of those that can change your entire life. Highly Recommended!!!

★★★★★ Must read!

An essential book for Christians. An insightful book on spirituality and circumstance.

★★★★★ Great read!

I thought this was a fantastic book. The author made strong points and backed it with clear concise thoughts. The reading was easy and thought-provoking. Highly recommend to all those interested in philosophy and religion. Easy to read and very thought-provoking! Candido masterfully weaves philosophy and religion together in captivating manner. Highly recommend!

★★★★★ A real gem!

It is often said that Dynamite comes in small packages. This is an example that makes the "cliché". An articulate weaving of spiritual and practical knowledge. In fact, you learn, if you didn't know already, that the spiritual truth of God is the most practical of all. If you already knew, you are reinforced and motivated to action in any endeavor in which you are involved. Segarra's writing will increase clarity, confidence and purpose in your life all in a very quick read that you will enjoy and want to read over and over.

★★★★★ **Unique, enlightening book!!**

This book bought to light issues of deep, penetrating thought. It truly makes you think! Possibilities of personal growth are endless! Worth the read!

★★★★★ **A must read**

Written in such a way that it gives you a spiritual awakening of your thought pattern. I highly recommend this book.

★★★★★ **Very Engaging**

This book helps you see beyond your immediate problems and see the 'bigger picture.' This book will help you to see the timeless principles in the Bible and then apply them to your life.

★★★★★ **Fantastic**

A book with a great blend of spiritual truths and practical thought.

OTHER BOOKS BY CANDIDO SEGARRA...

A HANDBOOK ON BECOMING A TRUE PROFESSIONAL

How to develop the Disciplines & Attributes
that will make you a TRUE PROFESSIONAL

CANDIDO SEGARRA

★★★★★ From the author of the acclaimed book
Are You the Architect of your Circumstances

Foresight Book Publishing™

A Revolution in Book Publishing
Turn Your Sermon Series Into A Book.

WWW.FORESIGHTPUBLISHINGNOW.COM

Foresight Management Development Program©

A world class management development training program to develop, equip and empower the best managers in America

www.ForesightMDP.com

www.ingramcontent.com/pod-product-compliance
Lightning Source LLC
Chambersburg PA
CBHW031300290426
44109CB00012B/664